# YOU DECIDE YOUR ADVENTURE

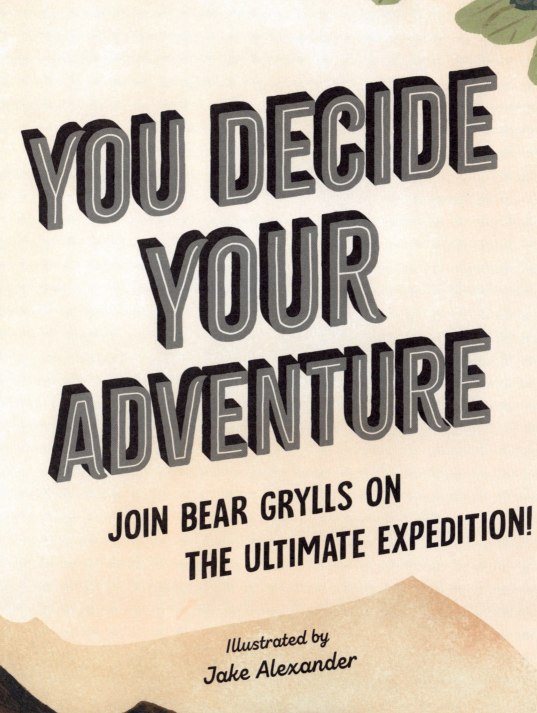

# YOU DECIDE YOUR ADVENTURE

## JOIN BEAR GRYLLS ON THE ULTIMATE EXPEDITION!

Illustrated by
Jake Alexander

# Contents

06 ..............................ABOUT YOUR ADVENTURE

08 ..............................WELCOME TO YOUR ADVENTURE

10 ..............................SETTING THE SCENE

12 ..............................EXPEDITION KIT

14 ..............................BEAR'S TOP TIPS: GETTING READY TO GO

28 ..............................BEAR'S TOP TIPS: NAVIGATING AT NIGHT

32 ..............................BEAR'S TOP TIPS: SETTING UP CAMP

42 ..............................BEAR'S TOP TIPS: FOOD IN THE WILD

46 ..............................CHECKPOINT 1: RIVER CROSSING

48 ..............................BEAR'S TOP TIPS: WATER OBSTACLES

60 ..............................CHECKPOINT 2: APPROACH THE MOUNTAINS

62 ..............................BEAR'S TOP TIPS: CLIMBING

72 ..............................BEAR'S TOP TIPS: FIRE

84 ..............................CHECKPOINT 3: EDGE OF THE VALLEY

86 .................................BEAR'S TOP TIPS: ABSEILING

92 .................................BEAR'S TOP TIPS: MAKE A SHELTER

94 .................................CHECKPOINT 4: MOUNTAIN BIKING

106 ...............................BEAR'S TIPS FOR ADVENTURE

108 ...............................GLOSSARY

# About your adventure

In this interactive adventure it's up to you to choose how you navigate your expedition. Throughout the book there will be choices to make. You'll know when it is time to make a choice when you come across a **choice box**.

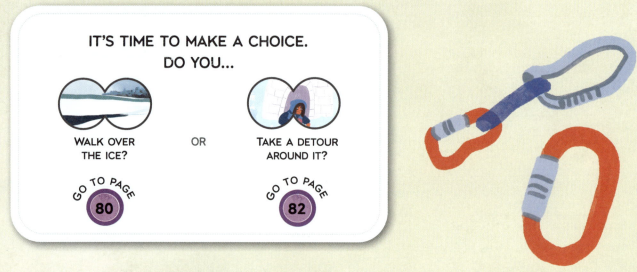

## MAP & CHECKPOINTS

But don't worry, before you head off into the wilderness you'll be armed with a map. The map will show you where you are aiming to go and the checkpoints along the way. At each checkpoint you'll find new kit to help you complete the next leg of your journey.

## SURVIVAL TIPS & TRICKS

You'll also find survival tips throughout that will teach you vital skills and help you complete your expedition. The tips and tricks will help you complete your adventure and arm you with vital survival skills.

### OVERHAND KNOT
*This knot can be used to tie two pieces of rope together.*

### FIGURE EIGHT
*This is an easy knot that is tied at the end of a rope to stop you slipping off the end of the rope when abseiling.*

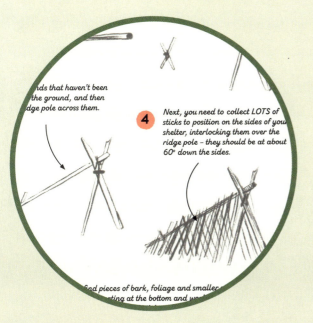

## ADVENTURE ANECDOTES

It might seem daunting, heading off into the wilderness, but don't worry, Bear is here to give you a hand. Throughout the book you'll find anecdotes from Bear's own travel journal—these will be packed full of advice for how to face the challenges up ahead.

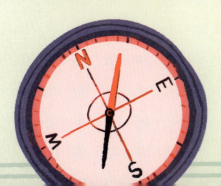

# Welcome to your adventure

Hello!

I'm Bear Grylls and I've got an adventure for you.

Sometimes life can feel out of your control, but in this expedition, YOU decide what happens. I'll be there to help guide you and give you some handy tips and tricks, but the decisions will be yours to make. You'll have four days to complete the expedition and make your way to the extraction point. Sounds simple, right? There's no reason why it can't be, as long as you make smart decisions along the way. So, if you feel up to the challenge, get ready to choose your own adventure...

Just like on a real adventure, you'll have to think fast. The choices you make will reveal which page you need to turn to in the book. Remember to choose carefully—at best you could overcome a challenging situation; at worst it will end your expedition.

So much of survival is about preparation—the better prepared you are, the better chance you have at success. But sometimes you'll need to be able to adapt and think on your feet.

Adventures can be as much of a workout for your brain as they are for your body. With all this in mind, it's time to turn the page to discover where you're heading...

Bear.

# Setting the scene

This adventure is in the Northern Hemisphere, so there'll be different terrains you'll need to face: snowcapped mountains, craggy cliffs, exposed grassland, dense forests, and even water obstacles. You'll also come across lots of wildlife—everything from rabbits and squirrels to wolves and bears.

As you'll see from your adventure map, you need to make your way to the highlighted extraction point. There are four checkpoints along the way that you'll need to reach before you can continue to the next stage. Some of these checkpoints will have extra pieces of kit that you might need for the next leg of the journey.

# Expedition kit

Here's your kit. Different adventures often require different items, depending on the terrain you'll encounter, but these eight items should cover the basic essentials you'll need for survival.

**WATERPROOF MATCHES**
These are the best thing to start a fire in harsh conditions.

**WATER PURIFICATION TABLETS**
The easiest and quickest way to make sure life-saving water is safe to drink.

**SNARE WIRE**
As well as catching food, snare wire can have lots of survival uses like lashing together sticks since it is very strong.

**A COMPASS**
To help you find your way.

**EMERGENCY CORD**
This can have so many uses: tying things, hauling heavy objects, constructing a shelter, fishing, first aid, etc.

**FIRE STARTER**
Any survival kit without this would be incomplete —it's always possible to make a campfire with this piece of equipment.

**MINI KNIFE**
Used for cutting, chopping, preparing and eating food, digging, carving, and lots more. But always remember to use a knife safely!

**LANYARD WHISTLE**
To signal for help if you are stranded and need search and rescue to hear you.

*This essential kit comes in a WATERPROOF BAG for protection against the elements.*

As well as all this, you'll have a tent, a sleeping bag, and a limited supply of food rations and drinking water. You won't be able to carry enough for all four days as this would weigh you down, so you'll find more rations at each checkpoint—if you miss a checkpoint, though, you are on your own.

Finally, it's important that you look after your kit—you never know when something could come in useful. If you lose anything along the way, it'll be gone for the rest of the adventure.

You have your map and your kit, so it's time to get started.

## Turn the page for some useful hiking tips

# BEAR'S TOP TIPS

## Getting ready to go

The big thing to remember is preparation, preparation, preparation. You need to prepare your kit, and this can take weeks. I like to set everything out in front of me. Things get added and things get taken away. You swap items for alternatives that are smaller or lighter. Sometimes you need to sacrifice things that would be nice to have, but are actually a luxury. On most expeditions, your kit will need to be under a certain weight, because it's going to go on packhorses, a sled, or carried on your own back.

Sometimes I take a regular toothbrush and hack off a bit of the handle before going on an adventure. It might not sound like much, but anything you can do to make your kit smaller and lighter helps. You might be used to using a knife, fork, and spoon, but when you're out in the wild, often just a spoon will do.

Personal admin is important, too—and I'm not talking about filing paperwork! You need to organize your kit. I like to keep everything in labeled waterproof bags in my rucksack: clothes, rations, first aid kit; everything has its place. There's nothing worse than sharing a tent with someone who doesn't have good personal admin and makes a mess—we call them tent sheet monsters!

## Now you're ready to turn the page...

# Navigating

You might not always be able to see your extraction point because of obstacles that block your line of sight or maybe you're just too far away. So, to get there, you're going to have to navigate using more than just sight alone.

Smartphones are excellent pieces of tech to help you find the best route between two points. They use satellites orbiting Earth to figure out exactly where you are with a global positioning system (GPS). However, to do this your phone needs to be charged and have a decent signal. If either of these are missing, you'll need to go old school...

It's time to check the map and put that compass in your kit to use—but to do that, you'll need to know how to use them.

## THERE ARE DIFFERENT TYPES OF COMPASS, INCLUDING:

**AIR-DAMPED COMPASS**—simple and cheap, with an approximate indication of magnetic north. The slightest movement makes the needle move. Best left at home and not taken on any hike or expedition.

**SIMPLE MAP-SETTING COMPASS**—a liquid-filled compass that shows magnetic north only. Often has a useful clip to attach it to the side of a map.

**PRISMATIC COMPASS**—extremely accurate, but tricky to use and pretty expensive.

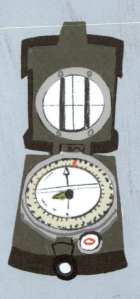

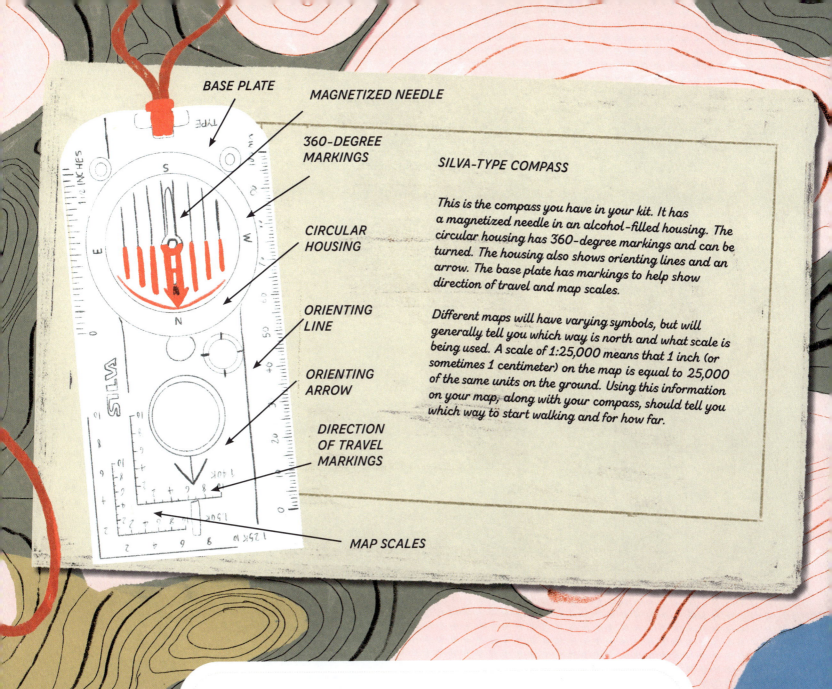

BASE PLATE

MAGNETIZED NEEDLE

360-DEGREE MARKINGS

CIRCULAR HOUSING

ORIENTING LINE

ORIENTING ARROW

DIRECTION OF TRAVEL MARKINGS

MAP SCALES

SILVA-TYPE COMPASS

This is the compass you have in your kit. It has a magnetized needle in an alcohol-filled housing. The circular housing has 360-degree markings and can be turned. The housing also shows orienting lines and an arrow. The base plate has markings to help show direction of travel and map scales.

Different maps will have varying symbols, but will generally tell you which way is north and what scale is being used. A scale of 1:25,000 means that 1 inch (or sometimes 1 centimeter) on the map is equal to 25,000 of the same units on the ground. Using this information on your map, along with your compass, should tell you which way to start walking and for how far.

## IT'S TIME TO MAKE A CHOICE. DO YOU...

HEAD OVER THE OPEN, BOGGY GROUND?

GO TO PAGE **18**

OR

STICK CLOSE TO THE TREE LINE?

GO TO PAGE **20**

# Open, boggy ground

Ever heard the phrase "don't get bogged down"? Well, it came from terrain like this—open, boggy ground. It might not look as dramatic as a rock face or a raging river, but it can be just as exhausting wading through this kind of environment.

Bogs are squelchy areas. The soft, spongy ground beneath your feet consists of decaying plant matter, known as peat, which can take thousands of years to form and often occurs in poorly drained lake basins. In this terrain, you will find yourself stepping or jumping over wet areas often, which will take a toll on your energy reserves. There's also more chance of slipping or falling than on dry ground, so you'll need to take your time with each step. Balance is key to successfully navigating your way across a bog.

TAKING THE TIME TO KNOW WHAT KINDS OF PLANTS ARE UNDER YOUR FEET CAN HELP, TOO. CAN YOU SPOT ANY OF THE FOLLOWING PLANTS AHEAD OF YOU?

*SPHAGNUM MOSS*—comes in a variety of colors and is a good indicator that you're entering wet ground. The light green stuff loves really wet ground and is best avoided. Red sphagnum moss tends to be in drier ground and will be better to walk on.

*WOOLLY FRINGE MOSS*—often found in dry, rocky areas.

*BOG COTTON*—often found in wet areas that also contain sphagnum moss. The name comes from its white cotton-like tufts; avoid areas where this grows.

*DEER GRASS*—grows in drier "stepping stone" areas called tussocks. These are safe to walk on.

*HEATHER AND BRACKEN*—another of nature's safe paths, these plants like dry ground, so can be useful.

## IT'S TIME TO MAKE A CHOICE. DO YOU...

FOLLOW THE HEATHER AROUND THE BOG?

OR

HEAD STRAIGHT ACROSS THE BOGGY GROUND?

GO TO PAGE **26**

GO TO PAGE **100**

# The tree line

You've reached the tree line. It's at this altitude that trees stop growing and give way to a rockier area as you ascend a mountain. Depending on where you are in the world, the tree line can start at different altitudes:

Scotland: 1,640 ft.

Canadian Rockies: 7,875 ft.

Yosemite National Park: 10,500 ft.

Swiss Alps: 7,220 ft.

Himalayas: 10,500–16,100 ft.

The tree line is often a sign that you're entering a harsher terrain. This can mean colder temperatures, low moisture, snow, and high winds. This can impact your expedition in a number of ways:

1. *YOU'RE MORE EXPOSED*—wind, rain, and snow will all be felt more intensely at this altitude.

2. *MORE DIFFICULT TO NAVIGATE*—with few identifiable features (you're basically just surrounded by gray rocks), you'll be relying more than ever on your compass and map.

3. *TRICKIER TERRAIN*—rocks can be unsteady, so you'll need to take extra care with each step you take.

An awareness of what's going on around you is key to a successful adventure. Your sense of hearing has just picked up on a noise coming from within the forest. There is a rustling sound like something is moving through the undergrowth. As well as rustling, you detect a moaning and huffing, too.

### IT'S TIME TO MAKE A CHOICE. DO YOU...

**CARRY ON AND STICK TO THE PATH?**

OR

**INVESTIGATE THE NOISE?**

GO TO PAGE **26**

GO TO PAGE **22**

# ⚠️ DANGEROUS WILDLIFE

So, you want to find out where that noise was coming from?

It turns out that it's a bear grazing quietly. But don't be fooled—while it looks distracted by something in the undergrowth, it might not be comfortable with you at such close quarters.

If a bear starts to sway its head or begins making noises that sound like huffing, moaning, popping, or growling, it is beginning to feel agitated. If a bear lowers its head and its ears go back, that is a possible sign of aggression.

When you come across a bear, it might stand on its hind legs. While this might sound scary and intimidating, it could just be that the bear wants to get a closer look at you. In general, when a bear has identified you as human, it will leave you alone and run away.

At this stage, it's important to remain calm and assess the situation. If the bear is acting calm and just curious, you might be able to give it a wide berth and leave the area. However, this bear is looking a little agitated, so a confrontation looks inevitable.

### IT'S TIME TO MAKE A CHOICE. DO YOU...

TRY MAKING A LOT OF NOISE TO SCARE THE BEAR?

GO TO PAGE **26**

OR

TURN AROUND AND RUN AWAY AS FAST AS YOU CAN?

GO TO PAGE **24**

# DANGER AHEAD

Unfortunately, you have made a choice that has put you in danger or at risk of injury. Maybe you tried to outrun a wild animal, or you've eaten something that has made you very sick. We all get things wrong sometimes and mistakes can happen to any of us. I have taken risks on lots of expeditions and sometimes they don't pay off.

**WHICH DANGER DID YOU ENCOUNTER?**

*Running away from wild animals.*

*Eating foods like holly berries.*

*Drinking water straight from a stream.*

*Heading off-route without a plan.*

*Scrambling down slopes.*

*Trying to outrun bad weather.*

The choices you made have put you in an unsafe position, so it's time to get help and call in the rescue team.

## Turn to page 100

# It's getting dark

Looks like you made a smart decision and are now safe to carry on with your adventure. While it's important to remain focused on getting to the extraction point, sometimes it's good to take a moment to appreciate what you can see around you.

The landscape up here is very different to what most of us see in our everyday lives. Everything from the ground under your feet to the plants growing around you and even the weather conditions can feel somewhat alien. New experiences enrich our lives and can give us memories and stories to tell that last a lifetime. Whenever you're outdoors, look around you, look up, notice the environment—you're bound to find something amazing and surprising wherever you are.

IT'S TIME TO MAKE A CHOICE.
DO YOU...

CARRY ON THE EXPEDITION IN THE DARK?

GO TO PAGE **28**

OR

SET UP CAMP FOR THE NIGHT?

GO TO PAGE **32**

# BEAR'S TOP TIPS

## Trekking through the night

There are some locations, like in the Arctic, where you wouldn't choose to trek at night because it's too cold. And in the jungle, it's pretty much impossible to travel at night—it's just too dark and you risk getting lost or injured. However, in hot locations, like a desert, you always trek at night to take advantage of the cooler temperatures and then rest during the day, chasing the shadows, looking for any shelter from the extreme heat.

The trick with traveling at night is remembering that your navigation needs to be good. You often can't see what's in front of you, so you need to trust your compass. Without one it's possible that you'll end up walking around in a circle—this is because we all have a dominant, stronger leg.

Making sure your night vision is adapted to the light levels is really important. This doesn't mean adjusting fancy goggles or a headset, but your own eyes. As the light starts to fade, our eyes begin to adjust, but it can take 30-40 minutes for our eyes to get fully used to the darkness. Once your eyes have adapted, avoid looking at anything bright like a phone, or even the moon and stars, because this can ruin your night vision. If you do need to look up, cover one eye—I find my night vision comes back much faster when only one needs to readjust.

**\*Remember, try and keep this information in mind after you turn the page.**

# Navigating at night

Attempting to navigate at night can be a lot of fun, so well done for wanting to try it out. In fact, humans have used the stars in the night sky to navigate throughout time—after all, stars have been around far longer than GPS, compasses, or even hand-drawn maps.

It's important to remember that the sky at night changes all the time since the world rotates and orbits the sun. Where you live in the world will also affect the stars that you can see.

As you are in the Northern Hemisphere, the first thing to do is find Polaris, also known as the North Star. It's the brightest star in the Ursa Minor constellation (but NOT the brightest in the sky), and is sometimes called the Little Bear or the Little Dipper. Polaris is found in the bear's tail. Polaris got its name because it appears within a degree of the Celestial North Pole, and appears not to move. So now you know which way is north.

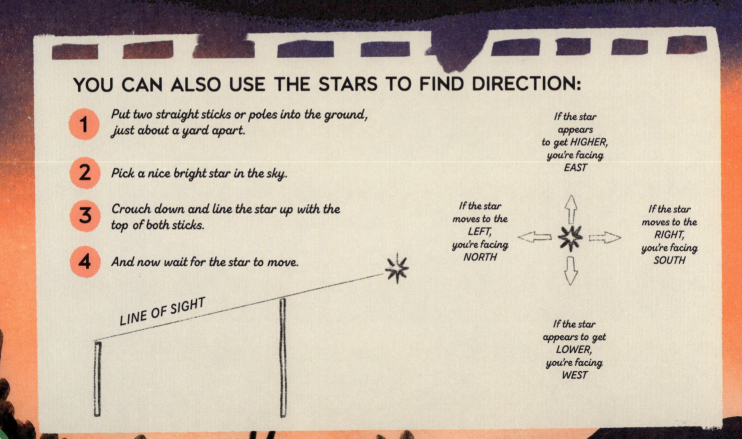

**YOU CAN ALSO USE THE STARS TO FIND DIRECTION:**

1. Put two straight sticks or poles into the ground, just about a yard apart.
2. Pick a nice bright star in the sky.
3. Crouch down and line the star up with the top of both sticks.
4. And now wait for the star to move.

LINE OF SIGHT

If the star appears to get HIGHER, you're facing EAST

If the star moves to the LEFT, you're facing NORTH

If the star moves to the RIGHT, you're facing SOUTH

If the star appears to get LOWER, you're facing WEST

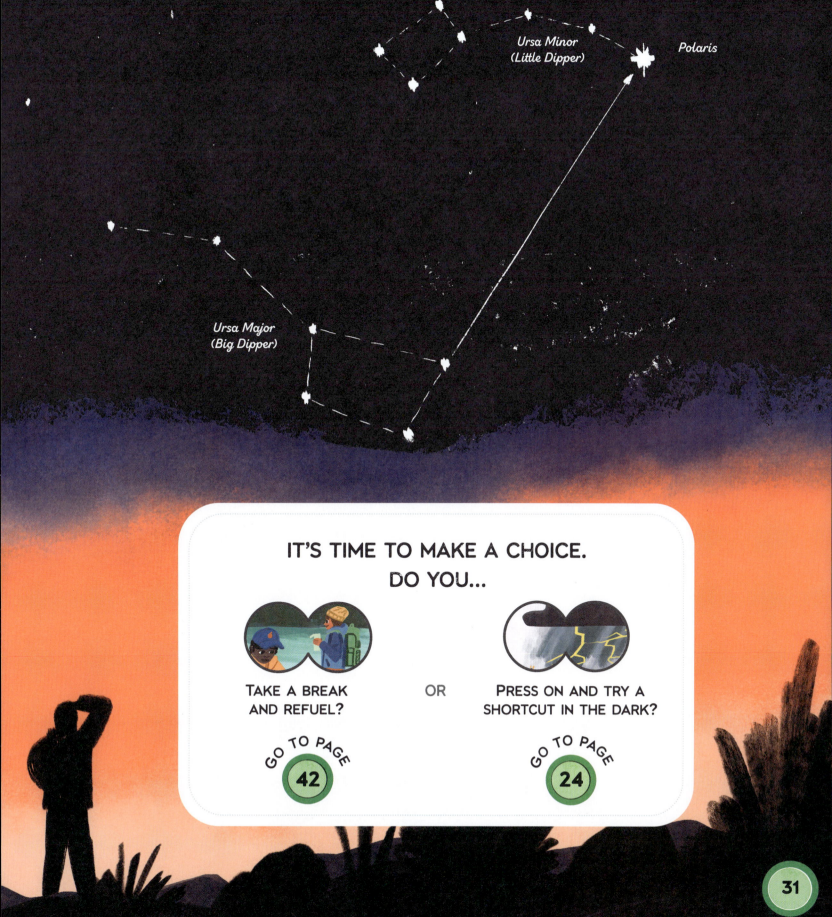

# BEAR'S TOP TIPS

## Setting up camp

When it comes to setting up camp, it's all about location, location, location. I always try and find somewhere flat that is near to water, but not so close that you could end up getting drenched—or even washed away!—by a flash flood. A source of local food is great—and I don't mean a supermarket! Whether it's bees with honey, sap trees that you can tap, plants you can eat, or even somewhere you can lay traps to catch something like rabbits, you will need a source of food.

I like to find somewhere with overhead coverage if possible. If you're in a forest or wooded area, make sure that they are healthy trees—you don't want any deadfall. Falling trees or branches can be incredibly dangerous.

When you've found somewhere flat to set up camp, try and find as many ferns and dry matter as you can. These will provide insulation under your tent and help to keep you as warm and comfortable as possible.

And make sure that your door is facing out of the wind—there is nothing worse than opening the door to cold wind and snow blowing in!

**To set up your camp, turn the page.**

# Choosing a campsite

Choosing to set up camp now is a good idea while there's still some light. It'll mean that hopefully you can get some rest tonight, and start tomorrow feeling refreshed and ready for the next leg of the adventure.

If you're lucky enough to be camping somewhere with an official campsite, you'll have access to tried and tested areas to pitch your tent, as well as basic amenities. But out here in the wild, it's up to you to select a suitable place to set up camp.

**HERE ARE SOME TIPS ON WHAT MAKES A GOOD PLACE TO SET UP CAMP:**

### DO...

- ✓ Find a sheltered spot if you are on high, exposed ground
- ✓ Move a bit higher up if you are on lower, wet ground
- ✓ Seek somewhere sheltered from the wind
- ✓ Check that there isn't a risk of rockfall or avalanche
- ✓ Find somewhere near a clean water supply
- ✓ Select an area that is reasonably flat and free of rocks and roots

### DO NOT...

- ✗ Camp where there's risk of flooding
- ✗ Set up in the bottom of valleys where there are pockets of colder air attracting frost and mist
- ✗ Be too close to water because there will also be lots of bugs
- ✗ Sleep under deadwood trees that could fall
- ✗ Camp under single trees that could attract lightning

IT'S TIME TO MAKE A CHOICE. DO YOU...

SET UP CAMP AT THE BOTTOM OF THIS SLOPING HILL?

GO TO PAGE 36

OR

SET UP CAMP HIGHER UP ON FLAT, ELEVATED GROUND?

GO TO PAGE 42

# Bad night

That was not the restful night's sleep you'd been hoping for. The wind and rain were relentless and not only was the rain pelting your tent, it was also running off the hill and straight toward your camp. Your tent has taken a real battering and now you and all your kit are completely soaked.

Pitching your tent in low-lying areas like ditches or valleys might seem like a good idea in good weather as you're less exposed. It might even feel like the sensible choice in bad weather to provide some shelter. However, it can often make your situation much worse!

Areas like this can fill up quickly with water, which means so will your tent. And that will lead to you and your gear getting soaked, too.

It's times like this that your morale can really begin to dip. You're going to need to show strength of character. You don't want to start the day's journey cold and wet, so it's time to take stock and warm up.

### Turn to page 38

# Warming up

Getting cold and wet in the outdoors is not ideal, but sometimes it's unavoidable. It's important to get yourself warm and dry as quickly as possible because at best you'll feel uncomfortable, but at worst you could develop hypothermia.

One of the best things you can do is only wear clothes made of quick-drying material and avoid things made of cotton—it'll really speed up the drying process.

To get dry, you're first going to have to wring out your clothes by hand, squeezing as much water out as possible. Then you need to hang them up to dry. If it's raining, you could put up a small clothesline in your tent or under a tarp.

If it has stopped raining, position your clothesline in a sunny spot with good airflow. The emergency cord from your kit strung between two trees would work really well. Otherwise, near your campfire is another good option—just make sure that it's not so close that there's a risk of your clothes catching on fire.

With your clothes now dealt with, that's a crucial new survival skill learned. Now it's time to get yourself warm. If you have a fire, make the most of its heat. Alternatively, keep active. Turn your body into a furnace and move around to help warm yourself up.

*Turn to page 40*

# Finding water

After a bad night's sleep, it's important to not forget about the essentials. And staying hydrated is key to your survival.

Water is essential to help your body function—both physically and mentally. However, it looks like you have used up all the water you brought with you. Luckily, you can hear the sound of running water and when you go to investigate, you find a stream with flowing water. The water looks crystal clear and appears to be coming down from the hill and heading toward the valley.

While rain on an adventure can cause lots of problems, like you and your gear getting wet, it also seems to have replenished this stream. Maybe your luck has changed! With a bit more investigation, the water looks pretty clean and free from any obvious dirt. In fact, it looks just like the tap water that you would drink straight from the kitchen sink at home.

## IT'S TIME TO MAKE A CHOICE. DO YOU...

**DRINK STRAIGHT FROM THE STREAM?**

GO TO PAGE **24**

OR

**USE ONE OF YOUR WATER PURIFICATION TABLETS?**

GO TO PAGE **42**

# BEAR'S TOP TIPS

## Food in the wild

You've been working hard and now it's time to think about food.

I always carry emergency rations; this could include a chocolate bar, dried fruit, and a packet of hydration salts I can add water to that's full of vitamins. These are all wrapped up in masking tape and in a waterproof bag and kept in the bottom of my backpack. They are only ever used in a real emergency—not after a few hours or even a day, but after a couple of days when a boost is required.

In the past, I have prepared snacks before heading out on an expedition. I'd unwrap some dried fruit and chocolate and put them in a bag and mix them all together. I'd keep this goody bag in my pocket and dip into it and have a handful at a time. There'd be no wrappers to take off or have to throw away, just a quick hit of energy.

Lots of ration packs I've used are boil-in-the-bag meals. Unfortunately, a side effect of the packs is that you get terrible constipation—once I didn't use the toilet for three days! However, there was often a hot chocolate in the ration packs, and these would have the opposite effect. On an expedition in Iceland once, it was about -13°F outside with winds blowing at 70mph, and within two minutes of drinking the hot chocolate, I had to race outside the tent to have a awfully chilly toilet break!

**To find out what's on the menu, turn to page 44**

# Choosing what to eat

It's time to think about having something to eat to boost your energy levels before the next stage. When you're on an adventure, you might find yourself tempted to try foraging for your own food to boost the limited supplies you've brought with you. It's a great skill to master, but it's important that you know what you're doing and what foods to look out for, and what to avoid.

## FORAGING DOS:

✓ Make sure you know what the plant is before you eat it

✓ Wash your harvest well before eating

✓ If cooking, make sure the food is steaming hot

✓ Only eat a small amount at first in case you have a bad reaction

✓ Keep some food aside so that it can be identified if you later become unwell

✓ Only take what you need, leave enough for other foragers and, more importantly, for wildlife

✓ Pick with care and avoid damaging or uprooting a plant

## FORAGING DON'TS:

✗ Don't forage alone without an adult who knows what they are doing

✗ Collect any plant or fruit that looks damaged or bruised

✗ Harvest food near an industrial site or busy road

✗ Choose plants low to the ground that may have been contaminated by animals

✗ Eat wild mushrooms

✗ Collect rare species or within restricted areas of National Parks

⚠ *REMEMBER, you should only forage if you are 100% sure it's safe to eat.

---

### IT'S TIME TO MAKE A CHOICE. DO YOU...

 EAT A HANDFUL OF HOLLY BERRIES?

GO TO PAGE **24**

OR

 USE ONE OF THE RATION PACK MEALS IN YOUR KIT?

GO TO PAGE **46**

# River crossing

**CHECKPOINT 1**

Good decision, and you've reached the first checkpoint! It looks like your reward for getting this far is a raft and equipment. And judging by the raging river in front of you, this has come at just the right time.

### LET'S TAKE A LOOK AT WHAT EQUIPMENT YOU'VE GOT:

**HELMET**
There are plenty of twists, turns, and drops through rocky rivers in rafting, so something to protect your head is essential.

**PERSONAL FLOTATION DEVICE (PFD)**
A buoyancy aid designed to give you a good range of motion while staying above water.

*DRY SUIT AND GLOVES*
To help keep you dry, regulate temperature, and keep you protected.

*THROWLINE*
A rope in a bag that will unravel when thrown.

*PADDLE*
Used to steer, stop, and propel your way through the water.

## IT'S TIME TO MAKE A CHOICE. DO YOU...

JUMP STRAIGHT INTO THE RAFT?

OR

TAKE A FEW MINUTES TO PREPARE FOR THE NEXT STEP?

GO TO PAGE **50**

GO TO PAGE **48**

# BEAR'S TOP TIPS

## Water obstacles

Water is unpredictable. It is unforgiving. It is super dangerous. And the worst are jungle rivers. They are full of vicious animals that might want to eat you. They are also full of debris, and what we call "river jungle furniture"—broken trees, things that are under the water that you can't see.

It's important to pick a decent entry point and to slide in rather than jump, but also look for where you will be exiting the water. You don't want to make it across a river and then not be able to get out because the bank is too steep. When you're swimming across a river, make sure you stay facing and swimming upstream; this way, you'll be swimming against the current as you glide across. You will need to identify an eddy—it's a still, flat area of water out of the current. You'll often find them behind a big rock. It means that you can have a brief rest and break the crossing into two parts.

On an adventure in Sumatra, I had checked out a river in the late afternoon before I planned to cross it the next morning. When daybreak came, the river was suddenly much faster and much deeper. I knew that the alternative was a long detour, so I made the decision to go in and power against the river. I spotted an eddy on the far bank and decided I'd head for that. I jumped in and the river was so ferocious that I was whooshed past the eddy and disappeared under the water! I eventually ended up exiting the river half a mile downstream. The lesson there was that water is strong, it is dangerous, and you should never underestimate it. Do NOT get in a river unprepared or alone—ever.

## Now turn to page 50

# Set off in a raft

Many rivers start high up in the mountains. Sometimes these rivers begin because of melting snow or because there's more rain. Some of this rain will soak into the ground, some will collect in pools and, with a little help from gravity, some will start making its way downhill, eventually reaching the sea.

What starts as a trickle can turn into a small stream, and when these small streams join up, faster-flowing rivers can form, and in some cases these rivers become dramatic rapids.

Up ahead there's a fork in the river, so you're going to need to make a decision, and quickly.

Do you head toward the fast and furious rapids, or would you rather follow the bend and see where that takes you?

# Navigate the rapids

So, you're a bit of an adrenaline junkie, are you? That can be the only reason you've chosen the rapids! Traveling through the water at high speeds is not for the faint-hearted. Only time will tell if greater risks lead to greater rewards...

You're going to have to harness all your strength to navigate along this river. With the water traveling quickly and in different directions, you're going to need to use your paddle to stay on course. The water is foaming up and it's easy to see why it's called white-water rafting now. You'll need to judge when to steer and when to paddle. It's important that you maneuver around any obstacles like large rocks or fallen trees because crashing into one of those could lead to you capsizing.

## RIVERS ARE GRADED FROM I TO VI:

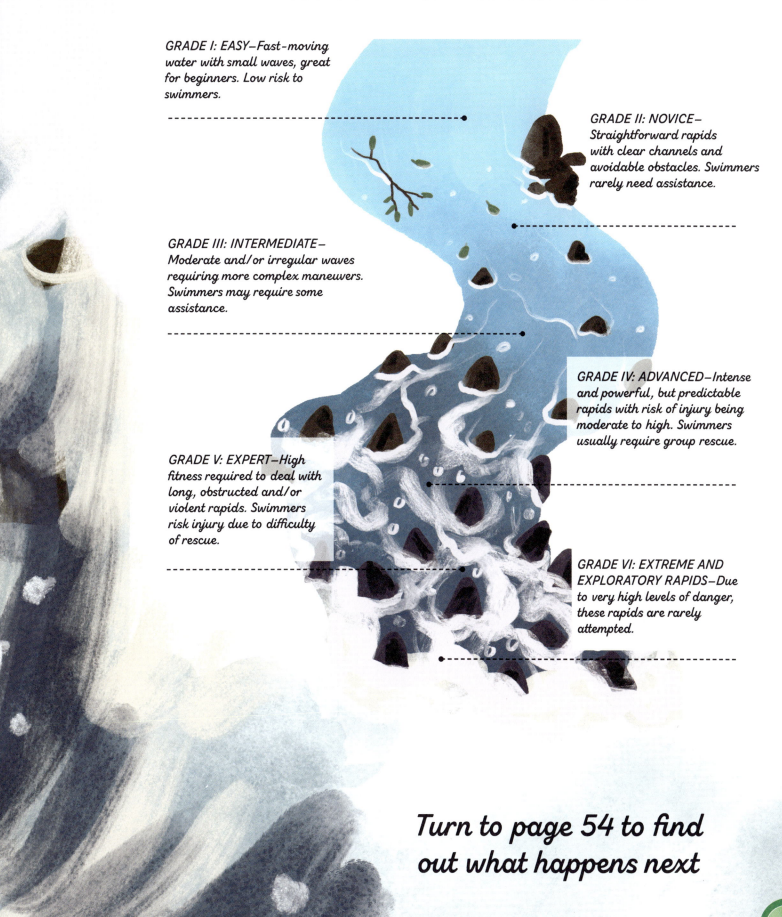

**GRADE I: EASY**—Fast-moving water with small waves, great for beginners. Low risk to swimmers.

**GRADE II: NOVICE**—Straightforward rapids with clear channels and avoidable obstacles. Swimmers rarely need assistance.

**GRADE III: INTERMEDIATE**—Moderate and/or irregular waves requiring more complex maneuvers. Swimmers may require some assistance.

**GRADE IV: ADVANCED**—Intense and powerful, but predictable rapids with risk of injury being moderate to high. Swimmers usually require group rescue.

**GRADE V: EXPERT**—High fitness required to deal with long, obstructed and/or violent rapids. Swimmers risk injury due to difficulty of rescue.

**GRADE VI: EXTREME AND EXPLORATORY RAPIDS**—Due to very high levels of danger, these rapids are rarely attempted.

*Turn to page 54 to find out what happens next*

# Capsize scenario

Disaster! Your raft has capsized! But now is not the time to panic. Try and keep a clear head. What you do next could save your life...

It's important to make sure that you aren't tangled up in anything—you don't want to get caught in the riverbed. Equipment like loose ropes could easily get trapped in rocks and you don't want to get dragged under. If possible, try and keep your paddle in your hands. It can help you swim and push you off rocks, getting you to a calmer stretch of water. It can also be used as a walking stick when you are able to wade through shallower water.

A really important white-water swimming technique to remember is aiming to float on your back with your feet at the surface pointing downstream. You also want to be slightly upstream of your raft—this will hopefully avoid you getting squashed between it and any obstacles in the river.

IT'S TIME TO MAKE A CHOICE.
DO YOU...

SIGNAL FOR HELP?

OR

TAKE STOCK AND GET YOUR BEARINGS?

GO TO PAGE 100

GO TO PAGE 56

# Survival priorities

Rather than signal for help, you've shown your courage and made the brave decision to push on. Some survival situations require lightning-fast reactions, whereas others like this one allow you more time to assess your next move.

First, check your pockets to see if you have anything of use. Next, have a look around you. There could be something in the immediate terrain that could come in handy.

## KNOW YOUR NUTS

All nuts are a source of energy and, like hazelnuts, lots can be eaten raw, including walnuts, sweet chestnuts, pine nuts, and beech nuts. However, you shouldn't eat too many at once as they can cause an upset stomach.

WALNUTS

HAZELNUTS

Hazelnuts are high in protein and are a source of vitamin E. They will give you vital calories after all the energy you used when your raft capsized. You just need to remove the green leaf casing with the brown outer shell and tuck in.

SWEET CHESTNUTS    PINE NUTS    BEECH NUTS

*Now that you've replenished your energy levels, turn to page 58*

# Navigate by nature

After the adrenaline rush of the white-water rafting, it's time to continue with your adventure on land. But with your kit washed away, you're going to need to figure out other ways to get to the extraction point.

Did you know that the watch on your wrist can help you figure out which way is north? If you live in the Northern Hemisphere, point the hour hand toward the sun. The halfway point between the hour hand and 12:00 is south, meaning the opposite is north. If you are in the Southern Hemisphere, point 12:00 toward the sun and the halfway point between that and the hour hand is north.

There's an even simpler method that doesn't require you to be wearing a watch.

## THIS IS THE SHADOW STICK METHOD:

**1** Find a straight stick that is about two feet long and poke it into the ground—you'll need somewhere in the open so that the stick casts a shadow.

**2** Put a rock at the end of the shadow.

**3** Wait for 20 minutes to allow the sun to move across the sky. If the shadow doesn't appear to have moved much, wait another 10 minutes or so.

**4** When the shadow has moved, place a second stone where the shadow now ends.

**5** Either draw a straight line or use another straight stick to connect the rocks.

**6** Mark the first stone with a W for west and the second stone with an E for east. Alternatively, you could scratch W and E into the ground next to each stone. This is because the sun moves from east to west across the sky.

**7** Put your left foot on the W and your right foot on the E. From this position you know that north is in front of you and south is behind you.

## Now you know which direction you're facing, turn to page 60

# Approach the mountains

**CHECKPOINT 2**

You've navigated the water and reached the next checkpoint. This time your reward is some climbing essentials. Faced with steep trails, cliff faces, and rocky mountains in front of you, it looks like it's going to come in handy soon.

## IN YOUR CLIMBING KIT YOU'LL FIND:

**CLIMBING SHOES**
The rubber sole and fit of the shoe will provide comfort and grip on rock.

**HARNESS**
This has multiple gear loops and a belay loop, with padding around your waist and adjustable leg loops.

**ROPE**
A 250-foot durable rope with an abrasion-resistant treatment.

**RUNNERS**
A pair of carabiners connected by a sewn sling called a "dogbone" that connect your rope to the rock face and will reduce your length of fall if you come off.

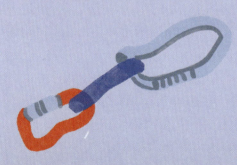

### LOCKING CARABINERS
Used to connect your belay device to your harness. It's crucial to use a locking carabiner during critical maneuvers like belaying or anchor cleaning.

### CHALK
Useful for absorbing the sweat from your hands and improving your grip.

### BELAY DEVICE
Attaches to your harness and helps control your descent by feeding the rope through the belay and creating friction.

### HELMET
Not only protects you in case of a fall, but also shields your head from rocks tumbling from above.

### CAMS OR "FRIENDS"
A safety device used for securing climbing routes.

---

## IT'S TIME TO MAKE A CHOICE. DO YOU...

JUMP RIGHT IN AND START THE CLIMB?

**GO TO PAGE 66**

OR

TAKE SOME TIME TO PREPARE?

**GO TO PAGE 62**

# BEAR'S TOP TIPS

## Climbing

Part of preparing for a climb at altitude is acclimatization—getting used to changes high up. You shouldn't just power straight up to 12,000 feet, but instead climb high, sleep low. This means that you might climb to 3,000 feet in a day, but then go back down 1,000 feet to find a place to sleep. And keep repeating this each day, eventually making it to the summit.

In all expeditions, it's important to travel light and move fast. You want to beat the weather, and you're more likely to reach your checkpoint quickly if you're not weighed down with excess kit.

As you know, the most important survival skill is often simply never giving up. But there are some occasions, especially when climbing a mountain, that you need to know when to pause and when to retreat. Maybe the weather forecast is bad or someone is sick. Remember: The mountain will always be there. If you come across a problem and need to abandon your climb, you can always come back. Sometimes you need to listen to your body and your instinct and put away your ego.

There are times when I use Alpine-style climbing. This means going lightweight and sometimes solo. Sometimes by being light and fast, it means we are more likely to succeed. Maybe we can move ahead of bad weather or avoid sleeping a night on the trail. Maybe it means less time, so there is less food to carry.

It's also important to pace yourself. Go steady and move efficiently. I've been in the Himalayas before and groups of people have raced past me, and then three or four hours later I've ended up overtaking them. They went off too fast and got sweaty, then stopped for a rest and ended up getting cold. They didn't acclimatize very well since they didn't give their bodies time to adjust. A steady pace where you don't stop can actually mean that taking it slow gets you there faster. The key is no sweat, get into a rhythm, and acclimatize properly. The Sherpas on an expedition continuously say "bistarai, bistarai"— slowly, slowly.

**Turn the page to begin the climb**

# Commence the climb

The mountainous part of the adventure is up ahead and the terrain is beginning to change.

Depending on where you are in the world, you might come across a rating system for hiking that can give you an idea of what to expect. In the USA, they use the Yosemite Decimal System, which ranks hikes across five classes, with Class 1 being the easiest and Class 5 being the most challenging.

CLASS 1—Easy routes on well-maintained and well-marked trails. Minimal technical equipment required, accessible for all levels and abilities of hiker.

CLASS 2—More challenging routes that are not as clearly marked. You might have to use your hands at times to steady yourself and could come across loose rock or steep scree.

CLASS 3—You'll be using your hands and feet at times to scramble across steep, rocky or snowy terrain.

CLASS 4—The most difficult terrain with steep and dangerous parts. You will find yourself using your hands and feet to navigate both up and downhill. You'll need a rope because falls could be fatal. You will probably also have a harness and helmet.

CLASS 5—At this level, you've moved from hiking to expert rock-climbing routes.

## STAY HYDRATED

When you're hiking at altitude, you'll also need to stay hydrated. Your body reacts to the decrease in oxygen at this level by increasing respiration and heart rate, meaning your body will be using more water. It's estimated that you need an extra 2-3 pints of water daily.

3 pints     3 pints     3 pints

Turn to page 68

# The climb begins

As you begin to scale the mountain, it looks like the next challenge could be out of your control... You've been making steady progress, climbing higher and higher, carefully picking out the best footholds as you go. It's tough going, so it's time to catch your breath. As you pause to take in the view, you notice dark clouds forming on the horizon... Could this mean trouble ahead?

When you are out in the wild, the weather can change very quickly. You are at the mercy of the elements out here, so you don't want to get caught out. Reading the weather is a crucial survival skill. Right now, you need to understand what type of clouds you're dealing with, spot what direction they're traveling in, and think fast.

**CAN YOU IDENTIFY THE INCOMING CLOUDS FROM THE FOLLOWING CLOUD TYPES?**

*CIRRUS CLOUDS*—thin and wispy clouds that look a little bit like feathers. Found at high altitudes, they usually mean the weather is about to change, but they rarely bring rain.

*CUMULUS CLOUDS*—very large puffy white or gray clouds that fill the sky. White clouds mean it will be dry, but when they are dark, expect rain.

*STRATUS CLOUDS*—thick clouds that appear to blanket the sky, blocking out any blue. If they are near the ground, they produce fog.

*NIMBUS CLOUDS*—"nimbus" is added to the names of clouds when there is rain or snow falling from them, like cumulonimbus, which is a looming, gray storm cloud. Be prepared for heavy rain.

IT'S TIME TO MAKE A CHOICE.
DO YOU...

TRY TO OUTRUN THE STORM?

GO TO PAGE
24

OR

SEEK SHELTER UNTIL IT PASSES?

GO TO PAGE
70

# Approaching dusk

The climb has taken you longer than expected. You look up at the sky and notice that the sun is beginning to go down.

If you're out in the wild and don't have a watch, knowing when it will get dark can be an important survival skill. You can do this with just the sun, the horizon, your own hands, and some basic math.

**1** *Start by locating the sun. You'll need to find somewhere on high ground without any trees or objects between you and the sun.*

**2** *Next, fully extend an arm and hold up your hand so that the palm is facing you. Position your little finger so that it is parallel with the horizon—the flat line between the sky and the ground.*

**3** Now, put your other hand on top of your first hand with both palms facing you. Tuck your thumbs in so that the index finger of your first hand is in line with the little finger of your second hand.

Then, if necessary, stack your first hand on top of your second hand, making sure that your second hand doesn't move. Keep track of the number of times you've stacked your hands on top of each other.

**4** Keep doing this until the hand on top reaches the sun. Each hand represents one hour, so if you've stacked your hands three times between the horizon and the sun, it's three hours until sunset.

**5** You can be even more precise and break this down into 15 minutes because each of your fingers represents 15 minutes. So, one hand and one finger between the horizon and the sun would be one hour and 15 minutes.

By using this trick, you've worked out that you have less than 45 minutes until sunset.

## IT'S TIME TO MAKE A CHOICE. DO YOU...

**SEEK SHELTER AHEAD?**

OR

**PRESS ON?**

GO TO PAGE **70**

GO TO PAGE **24**

69

# Seek shelter

Seeking shelter as the sun goes down is a good idea. It's important to make sure you're safe and it'll give you a chance to rest and assess what to do next. If you don't have access to a tent, there are a number of natural shelters that could provide protection from the elements:

*EVERGREEN TREES—These provide good protection from the sun and partial protection from wind, rain, and snow due to their conical shape and dense foliage.*

*FALLEN LOGS AND TREES—A fallen tree and its roots can provide a place to shelter with a small level of protection.*

*HOLLOW TREES—In the past, some humans lived in hollow trees. They aren't easy to come across, but if you do find one, it can be a good place to get some rest.*

THICKETS—Areas of evergreen vegetation can deflect bad weather in the winter, or provide a canopy from the hot summer sun.

CAVES—One of the oldest human "homes," these structures protect from wind and rain, and have a stable temperature. However, it's important to remember that other living creatures might also seek shelter in caves, the air can be poor, and caves can collapse.

ROCK OVERHANGS—Some of these can be almost the size of a cave, whereas others barely give you room to lie down.

## IT'S TIME TO MAKE A CHOICE. DO YOU...

SHELTER IN A CAVE AND START A FIRE?

GO TO PAGE **72**

OR

DECIDE THAT IT'S TIME TO SIGNAL FOR HELP?

GO TO PAGE **100**

71

# BEAR'S TOP TIPS

# Fire

A successful fire is vital for survival. There's so much that fire can give you. You can cook food on it, boil your water, make tools, and even deter predators. And a good fire gives you even more than all this—it also gives you good morale, and that in the wild is vital. When it comes to starting a fire, remember to BE prepared, BE persistent, and sometimes be ready to think out of the box.

There are the three elements that all fires need: heat, oxygen, and fuel. Collectively, they are known as the fire triangle. If one of these is missing, it's game over before you've even begun.

The key to successful fire making is PREPARATION—you need everything in place before you start: tinder (to take the initial spark), kindling (to get the fire going), and bigger fuel (to keep the fire burning). But don't smother your fire—look after your fire and it will look after you.

Tinder          Kindling          Fuel/logs

Always remember that fire can be dangerous. You should make sure that the fire is fully extinguished before you leave it. If there isn't any water nearby, one way to do this is to pee on it!

*Turn to page 74*

Sheltering in the cave has given you time to plan your next move. And to do this, you need to be calm.

The 5-4-3-2-1 method can help reduce lots of thoughts buzzing around your head, and give you time to focus. This technique can help to calm your mind in all sorts of situations, not just when you're on an adventure. Looking after your mental well-being is an important skill to master.

### SIGHT
*Spot five things that you can see. In the wild there will be lots of things: an impressive tree, an unusual rock formation, a cloud shaped like a rabbit, etc.*

### TOUCH
*Find four things that you can touch. Maybe you can find a smooth pebble or a crunchy leaf.*

### HEAR
*Note three things that you can hear: birdsong, the wind rustling in the trees, running water, etc.*

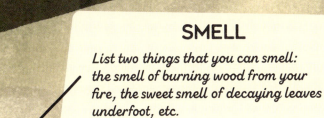

## SMELL

*List two things that you can smell: the smell of burning wood from your fire, the sweet smell of decaying leaves underfoot, etc.*

## TASTE

*Notice one thing that you can taste. Can you still taste the last snack you ate or is there something edible to hand?*

Now that you are at one with your environment and your senses are heightened after practicing the 5-4-3-2-1 technique, you hear a noise coming from the back of the cave. It's too dark to see anything, so you need to think carefully about what you do next.

### IT'S TIME TO MAKE A CHOICE. DO YOU...

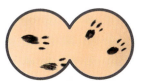

INVESTIGATE THE NOISE?

OR

FEEL IT'S TIME TO MOVE ON?

GO TO PAGE 76

GO TO PAGE 78

# Animal tracks and clues

So, you've decided to investigate? Being curious is a great skill for any adventurer—it's better to be aware than unaware of any dangers. Rather than head straight to the back of the dark cave, it could be useful to see if there are any signs near the entrance like animal tracks.

### RABBIT
*APPEARANCE—A pair of long, thin prints and a pair of shorter prints—this is because rabbits' back feet are much larger than their front feet. They have four pads on each foot.*

*SIZE—Front feet are about 1.5 inches long and 1 inch wide. Their back feet are twice as long, but they don't place their whole back foot down when running.*

## DEER
*APPEARANCE*—Each hoof leaves a distinctive long narrow imprint with a gap between them.

*SIZE*—This varies with species—a small muntjac will leave a footprint that is only 1 inch long and 0.75 inches wide, whereas a large red deer will have a footprint that is 3.5 inches long and 2.75 inches wide.

## WOLF
*APPEARANCE*—The toe prints are oval-shaped with a claw mark in front of each one. The main pad has a lobe shape at the front.

*SIZE*—Front feet are 3.5-5 inches in length and 3-5 inches in width, with the back feet being slightly smaller; that's about the same size as a human handprint.

Looking at the tracks you have discovered outside your cave, it seems there's a good chance that it could be wolves back there.

*It's time to move on and head to page 78*

# Navigating in snow

It's turning colder and it looks like the sky is filling with a cloud formation called altostratus. These clouds are at mid-levels in the sky and appear to be grayish-blue in color. They are made of dense ice crystals and water droplets that will fall as either rain or snow depending on the temperature.

At temperatures between -40°F and 32°F, water vapor crystallizes around pieces of dust in the clouds. When they become heavy enough, they fall to the ground. As they descend, the ice crystals join up with each other to form snowflakes. Some snowflakes can contain up to 100 ice crystals.

It is said that each snowflake is unique, but they can be divided into seven basic shapes:

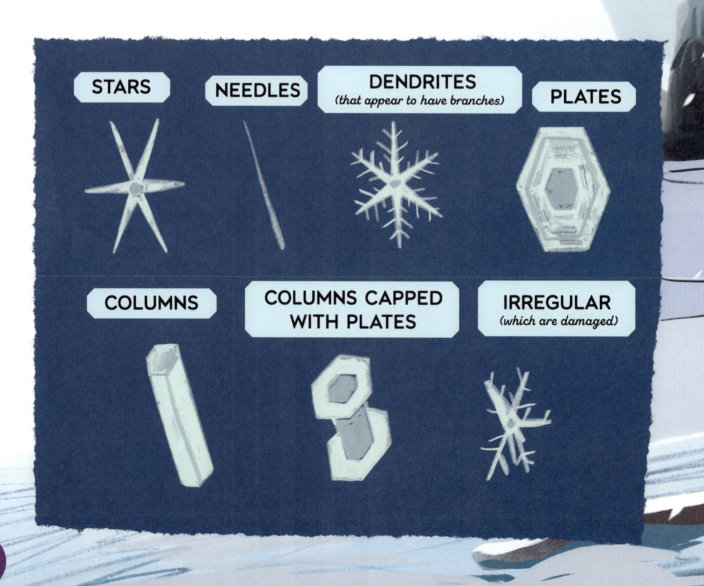

STARS

NEEDLES

DENDRITES
*(that appear to have branches)*

PLATES

COLUMNS

COLUMNS CAPPED WITH PLATES

IRREGULAR
*(which are damaged)*

When there has been snowfall, it can make navigating more difficult, but not impossible. If there are trees nearby, check to see if lichen is growing on them. There will be more lichen on the parts of a tree that face south.

Look at the trunks of trees and see if snow has stuck to one side. This will indicate which direction the snow-bearing wind came from, which will generally be from the north and east.

It looks like you need to go straight ahead, but this will mean crossing a frozen lake.

IT'S TIME TO MAKE A CHOICE.
DO YOU...

WALK OVER THE ICE?
GO TO PAGE 80

OR

TAKE A DETOUR AROUND IT?
GO TO PAGE 82

# Ice breaks

This could prove risky, but you've decided to take the direct route and cross the frozen lake.

Depending on the conditions, it is possible to safely walk on a lake that has frozen over, but there are some key things you have to remember:

**BE PREPARED**
*You will need to be wearing snowshoes or skis—both help to distribute your weight over a wider area, making the ice less prone to cracking. You should also be wearing warm clothes and carry snow picks—or ice axes—and a rope with you. And remember: Never attempt to cross a frozen body of water alone, always do it in a group. You should walk about 50 feet apart so that if one person goes in, the whole group won't follow and can then organize a rescue.*

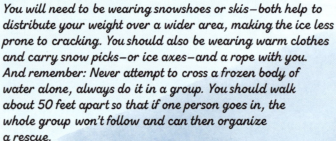

**STUDY THE ICE**
*Not all ice is the same, and the color of the ice can tell you a lot about it. Clear, blue ice is the strongest, and safest, to walk on. You should avoid white or black ice that can be thin and weak.*

### 3 MEASURE THE ICE

*Every 50 yards you should use your ice pick to measure the depth of the ice. 4 inches of clear, newly formed ice will be able to support you walking on it.*

3 in. UNSAFE!
4 in. Safe for one person
5–6 in. Safe for a small group

### 4 IF YOU FALL IN

*Keep your clothes on, but lose your snowshoes or skis. Make your way to the place the ice broke and put your hands on the ice while kicking your legs. Use your ice pick to claw your way out, and then roll away to solid ice—rolling distributes your weight better. Change your clothes and get warm. If you have no dry clothes with you, roll in the snow to get rid of excess water to help you dry faster.*

Despite not having the right kit, you press on and walk on the ice—but not for long, as the ice breaks and you fall in! You manage to struggle out of the icy waters and need to signal for help.

## Turn to page 100

# Build a snow shelter

Taking the detour around the frozen lake was the right choice to make. But the extra distance you've covered has drained your energy reserves, so it's time to rest. To do that, you are going to need to make a shelter.

Traditional snow buildings have been used for thousands of years by cultures used to freezing conditions.

## IGLOOS

*ORIGIN*—Used widely, but traditionally by Indigenous peoples of Canada's Central Arctic and the Qaanaaq area of Greenland.

*CONSTRUCTION*—Blocks of hard snow cut from the ground using saws and machete-like blades, arranged in a dome shape.

*USE*—Temporary home when away on hunting trips.

*SIZE*—9-12 feet high and 12-15 feet in diameter, large enough to house a family. Larger igloos can accommodate up to 20 people, whereas smaller ones can be used for a night or to provide shelter from a storm.

## SNOW CAVES

*ORIGIN*—Unknown, used by Indigenous peoples in cold regions for centuries.

*CONSTRUCTION*—A shelter dug into snow, with an entrance below the main space to retain warm air.

*USE*—Temporary housing for up to several nights while on an expedition.

*SIZE*—Large enough to house two to four people—any larger and construction becomes a long and difficult process.

## QUINZHEES

*ORIGIN*—Canada.

*CONSTRUCTION*—A large pile of loose snow that is collected and then shaped and hollowed. It should sit for two hours after construction to allow for the snow crystals to bond together. The interior is melted and then left to refreeze to strengthen the dwelling—this can be done by a lamp, candle, or even body heat.

*USE*—Short-term habitation.

*SIZE*—5-6.5 feet high in a dome shape, with a 10-13 foot diameter. Tall enough to sit or crouch in, but not stand.

With your limited equipment, you decide to make a small snow cave.

## Turn to page 84

## CHECKPOINT 3
# Edge of the valley

Well done, you've made it to checkpoint 3. Not only that, but if you look carefully into the distance, the extraction point is now within sight. There's just one problem: Between you and the extraction point is a deep valley with a sheer drop of about 150 feet.

### IT LOOKS LIKE YOUR NEXT SET OF EQUIPMENT MIGHT COME IN HANDY SOON:

**HARNESS**
A simple abseiling harness will have a waist belt, two leg loops, and a belay loop.

**PROTECTION DEVICES**
Used to secure your rope to an anchor like a rock. They can be wedged between rocks and are incredibly strong and durable.

**CARABINERS**
Useful for attaching things together.

### ROPE
This is the most essential piece of kit when it comes to abseiling; without it, you aren't going anywhere. Regular climbing ropes vary in diameter between about 0.3 and 0.45 inches. Thinner ropes are obviously lighter to carry and run more quickly through belay devices, whereas thicker ones are heavier but cause more friction and are more durable.

### BELAY DEVICE
By causing friction, belay devices allow you to control the speed of your descent. They come in two main categories: manual devices that you control yourself, and assisted breaking devices that have mechanical features to control your speed.

### HELMET
Used to protect your head from bumps and any falling debris.

Turn to page 86

# BEAR'S TOP TIPS

## Abseiling

In abseiling and rappelling, selecting where you're going to anchor your rope is essential. In an emergency situation, you would just tie your rope in one place. Best practice is two minimum, in case one anchor fails. Three would be the gold standard. Ideally, you want them at 90° to each other and then you're ready to begin your descent.

Unless you're in a life-threatening hurry, you don't want to bounce quickly down a rock face. Abseiling or rappelling is a mini expedition in itself. Better to pick your way down at a walking pace, looking left and right, avoiding debris and loose objects.

On one expedition I kicked off a huge rock that was loose. I shouted, "Rock below!" to warn anyone at the bottom of the rock face. As I carried on down, I came to a section of rope that the rock had obviously hit on the way down—it had cut through the rope. The white innards of the rope were visible through the black exterior layer. Luckily, the rope had been cut only a few yards from the

bottom of the descent and I could safely drop off the end and land on my feet. Otherwise, that would have been a tricky, potentially life-threatening situation. Many climbers have lost their lives abseiling off the end of a rope that wasn't long enough. That's why it's a good skill to tie a knot in the end of the rope to prevent this happening.

**Time for you to carry on, turn to page 88**

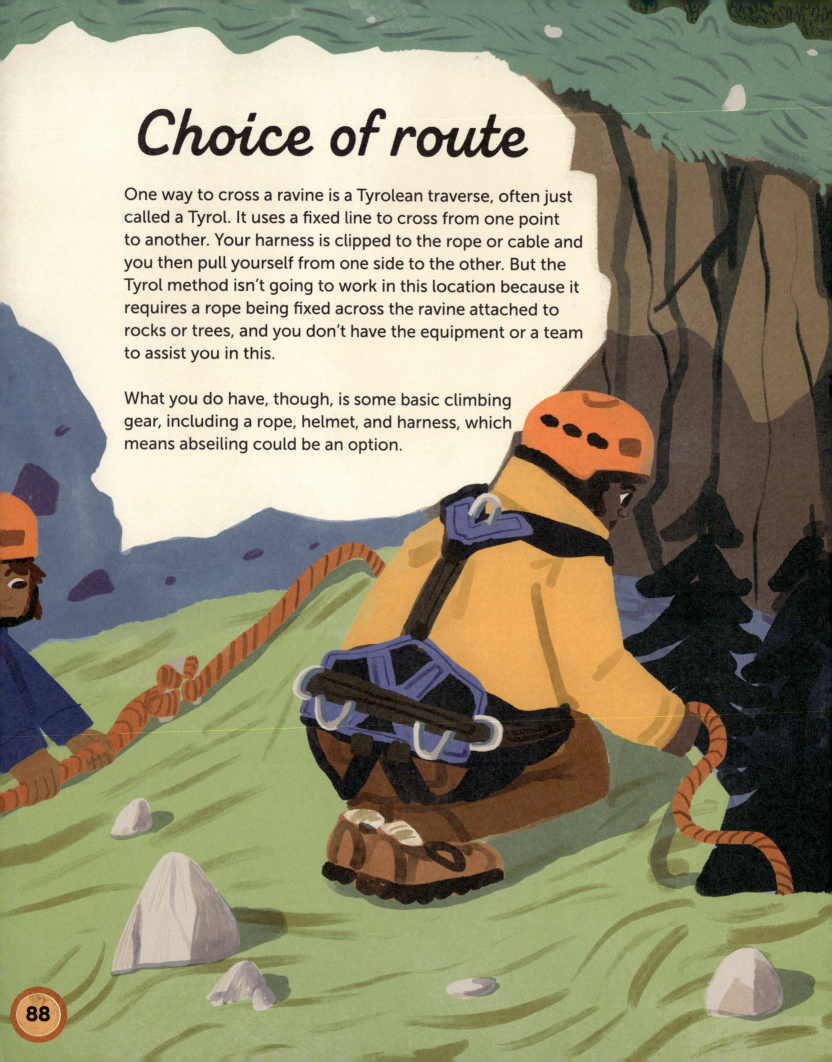

# Choice of route

One way to cross a ravine is a Tyrolean traverse, often just called a Tyrol. It uses a fixed line to cross from one point to another. Your harness is clipped to the rope or cable and you then pull yourself from one side to the other. But the Tyrol method isn't going to work in this location because it requires a rope being fixed across the ravine attached to rocks or trees, and you don't have the equipment or a team to assist you in this.

What you do have, though, is some basic climbing gear, including a rope, helmet, and harness, which means abseiling could be an option.

Knowing how to tie a knot can be vital in the wild. If you are thinking about abseiling, here are a few you should know:

### BOWLINE
*This knot is used to make a loop in the end of a rope that will not slip. It is invaluable in rescue situations, so learn it until you can tie it with your eyes closed, or even with one hand.*

### OVERHAND KNOT
*This knot can be used to tie two pieces of rope together.*

### CLOVE HITCH
*This adjustable knot is used to attach a rope to an anchor point like a pole.*

### FIGURE EIGHT
*This is an easy knot that is tied at the end of a rope to stop you slipping off the end of the rope when abseiling.*

The other option if you don't want to attempt abseiling would be to scramble down unaided.

---

## IT'S TIME TO MAKE A CHOICE. DO YOU...

**DECIDE TO ABSEIL?**

GO TO PAGE **90**

OR

**DECIDE TO SCRAMBLE?**

GO TO PAGE **24**

89

# Shelter

Abseiling down was a good choice, but tiring. Constructing a shelter down here while it is still light would be a good idea, but without any kit, options are limited. There are trees nearby, though, that could come in handy.

There are various shelters that can be built without any tools, including teepees and one-sided shelters. Here's how to construct a third option—an A-frame shelter:

**1** *Find a long, straight, sturdy stick that is taller than you (this will mean your finished shelter is long enough for you to lie down in). This will be your ridge pole.*

**2** *Collect two tall sticks of similar length and two shorter sticks of similar length. Bind each pair together using rope or thin vines to create a Y shape.*

**3** *Wedge the ends that haven't been joined into the ground, and then lie your ridge pole across them.*

**4** *Next, you need to collect LOTS of sticks to position on the sides of your shelter, interlocking them over the ridge pole—they should be at about 60° down the sides.*

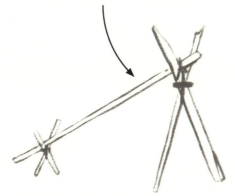

**5** *You now need to find pieces of bark, foliage, and smaller sticks and twigs to lie over your shelter, starting at the bottom and working your way toward the ridge pole. Ideally, this "blanket" should be about a foot thick.*

## Now turn to page 92

# BEAR'S TOP TIPS

## Make a shelter

It's important that you get out of the wind and rain. And remember not to go too big with your shelter—it only needs to be big enough for you and anyone you're traveling with. Not only will large structures take longer to construct, but they will also take longer to heat. Insulation is important, too. It can be the shabbiest shelter in the world, but as long as you have good insulation and it keeps you warm and dry, you'll be thankful. Keep it small, secure and use natural materials around you.

There was one night near Mount Washington, in New Hampshire, where I slept out in only a pile of leaves. These leaves had been swept by the wind into a bank, and I simply gathered them all together into a pile about a three feet thick. I pulled all the leaves over me and I actually had a pretty warm night. It was dry, and the trapped air between all the leaves kept me warm. Remember: Air is the best insulator. Maybe hibernating hedgehogs are on to something!

Once you've had a chance to get some rest in your shelter, it's time to continue on your adventure.

## Turn to page 94

# Mountain biking

You've made it to the final checkpoint of your adventure and waiting for you is a mountain bike and equipment… and right now, it's a smart option to get you to your extraction point.

**ALONG WITH YOUR BIKE, YOU'LL FIND:**

*MINI PUMP*
*Tires go flat, and a mini tire pump is a lightweight piece of kit to remedy this.*

*HELMET*
*To protect your head in case you come off your bike.*

**PUNCTURE REPAIR KIT**
A damaged tire would mean the end of your journey, so a quick way to repair it is essential.

**GOGGLES**
To protect your eyes from the sun and any debris that gets thrown up.

If this was a planned ride, you might take along things like energy snacks, a multi-tool, and a GPS tracker, along with wearing appropriate clothing and footwear. But today, these luxuries aren't available, so it's time to cycle on.

## Turn to page 96

# Continue along the trail

You're on your bike and heading toward the extraction point with spirits high. Here are five top tips to remember to get the most out of your mountain-biking experience:

**1 BODY POSITION**
You need to be in the "ready" position with your heels down, wrists down, arms and legs slightly bent, and head looking up toward where you're going, NOT at the front wheel.

**2 CORNERING**
It's important you set your speed before entering a corner, so brake before you get to a corner. Your head, shoulders, and hips should follow the line of the turn, all of which give you better weight distribution. And try to keep your pedals level to avoid obstacles.

**3 CLIMBING**
If it's a long climb, try lowering your saddle to help keep you centered. But keep your head up! You need to be able to see what's ahead of you like roots, corners, and loose ground. Avoid changing the gears too much—pick one and try to stick with it. This is all about control.

**4 BRAKING**
Be smooth with your braking. If you're hard and jerky, it can upset the balance of your bike. Use both brakes—using the front brake is key to avoiding skidding, especially downhill. Also remember when NOT to brake: mid-corner, across roots, or over rocky terrain.

**5 DESCENDING**
Going downhill can be thrilling, but avoid stooping low and stay tall. Stay smooth on your brakes and try not to brake sharply as this could lead to you coming off and injuring yourself.

You come to a part of the track that looks like it's heading away from your extraction point. The alternative is to attempt to bike off-road through the trees.

## IT'S TIME TO MAKE A CHOICE. DO YOU...

**CONTINUE ON THE TRACK?**
GO TO PAGE 104

OR

**HEAD OFF-ROAD?**
GO TO PAGE 98

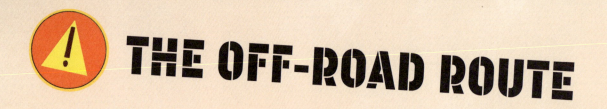

# THE OFF-ROAD ROUTE

Choosing to mountain bike off-road could not only see you injuring yourself, but it could also damage the environment and any wildlife that call it home. You should stick to marked trails that are maintained by organizations like the local national parks service.

Mountain bikers are at a much higher risk of fractures, dislocations, and concussions compared to on-road bikers. And this is increased further when venturing off trails and heading off-road though the woods. If you fall off and suffer a concussion, you are much more likely to be found on an official trail than in the woods.

It's always good to plan your route before you head out, but on this adventure it hasn't been possible. If you aren't able to research your route, you're better off sticking to a designated trail.

Choosing an off-road route and the hazards this could involve was an unnecessary risk, head to page 24

# Signal for help

Okay, so you've made a choice that has put you in a potentially dangerous situation. Even with the best preparation, there might be times when you find yourself in an emergency and you need to signal for help. Here's what to do...

**STAY CALM AND STAY PUT**
If you panic and wander around, it's more difficult for rescuers to find you.

**LOOK AROUND YOU**
Check around you for any landmarks to help get your bearings or retrace your steps.

**KEEP WARM**
You don't want hypothermia to set in, so dress in layers.

**DRINK WATER AND REST**
You need to stay hydrated and avoid overexertion.

**STAY VISIBLE**
Try to avoid covered areas and stay in the open.

**FOLLOW WATER**
If you can, follow a river or stream as this can often lead you to people.

### SIGNAL FOR HELP
This could be a whistle if you have one, flashing a light, a mirrored surface reflecting the rays of the sun, or building a fire. Try to make repeated signals of three (the international SOS distress call)—this could be three blows on a whistle or three flashes of a flashlight. If you're lucky, you will have a satellite phone or flare with you to signal for assistance.

### STAY POSITIVE AND MAKE SOME NOISE
Talking or singing to yourself can keep your spirits up, and it can also let anyone near you know you're there. Above all, be a true NEVER-GIVE-UPPER!

# Turn the page

# Rescue

You've reached the point where you need to be rescued. But you shouldn't feel too upset. It is important to take every experience as an opportunity to learn. Take a moment to look how far you have come and what you have achieved, rather than focusing on what you didn't manage to do on this occasion.

Even the most experienced of adventurers get into trouble and need to get help. This risk factor can be a thrill and can push you to achieve what you might have previously thought impossible.

Luckily, on this adventure you've been able to signal for help and a helicopter is on its way to rescue you. If you know that a helicopter is coming to rescue you, it's a good idea to make your way to clear, flat ground. This will allow the helicopter to hover over you or potentially even land. Depending on where you are, it can take hours or even days for a helicopter to reach you, but when you hear its engine approaching, the sense of relief can be overwhelming. If the helicopter can't land, you might need to be winched onboard. The cable sometimes makes you swing and spin as you rise up—don't panic—trust your rescuers to help you.

Safely in the helicopter, you can make your way back to base camp. And then it's up to you—will you take some time to regroup or choose to start your own adventure straight away again on page 8?

# You've made it!

**CONGRATULATIONS—YOU'VE MADE IT TO THE EXTRACTION POINT!**

Your preparation, problem-solving skills, your winning survivor attitude, and good decision-making have led to your success. The sense of achievement at reaching any goal can be a massive boost, and you should relish this. You did it!

Spend a moment to take this in. From the beginning of this adventure when you got hold of your kit, along the trails you took, and the obstacles you encountered, you really have taken control and chosen your own adventure. You're a true survivor now!

Not just on adventures, but in life also, we come across many obstacles. Sometimes we best demonstrate our strength when everything is not going our way. Being able to cope when situations don't go as planned is a great survival skill. You've got that.

All that is left to work out now is… where will your next adventure take you?

*Bear.*

# BEAR'S TIPS FOR ADVENTURE

Please Remember What's First (PRWF) is a phrase that I always keep in mind when I head out on any kind of adventure.

These four letters stand for the order of priorities that you need to remember:

## P is for Protection
Think about your immediate surroundings. Assess any threats like hungry animals or extreme weather and protect yourself from them. Building a fire can be a good option to help with various problems.

## R is for Rescue
Start to think about how you're going to be rescued. Even if you've told people where you're heading, they won't know exactly where you are at any given time, so make yourself easy to be rescued. Smoke from your fire can alert people to where you are, or you could move to somewhere more open where you're easier to spot.

## W is for Water

Although we can survive two to three days without drinking, it's a good idea to try and find a source of water. And although I wouldn't recommend it, there have even been times I've had to drink my own pee—but only as a very last resort!

## F is for Food

We can survive much longer without food—up to two or three weeks! But just because we can last this long doesn't mean we have to.

Remember your foraging skills and maybe even think about turning over logs to find things like maggots to eat. One of my favorite snacks in the wild is nature's popcorn— mealworms cooked in a little water and sugar. The little critters blow up like popcorn and are delicious!

# Glossary

**ACCLIMATIZATION**
the process of adjusting to a new climate, environment, or situation.

**ADRENALINE**
a hormone that helps the body respond to stressful, dangerous, or exciting situations.

**ALTITUDE**
a measurement of how high something is above sea level, or Earth's surface.

**AMENITIES**
things that make life more comfortable or pleasant, for example, showers in a campsite.

**ASCEND**
to go up, climb, or rise.

**AVALANCHE**
a large amount of snow, ice, earth, or rock that moves quickly down a mountainside or steep slope.

**BUOYANCY AID**
a flotation device that helps a person stay afloat in water while allowing them to move freely.

**CAPSIZE**
to turn over in a boat.

### CARABINER
a metal clip that connects two things together, such as a rope and a harness; it is a common piece of equipment used in mountain climbing.

### CONSTELLATION
a group of stars that form a recognizable pattern in the night sky.

### CONSTRUCTION
the process of building something.

### CONTAMINATED
something that has been made impure, dirty, or dangerous by adding something harmful or undesirable.

### DEBRIS
the remains of something that has broken down.

### DETOUR
a longer, less direct route to a destination.

### EDIBLE
something that is safe to eat, regardless of taste.

### EXPEDITION
a journey or trip that is organized for a specific purpose, such as exploring a new place or conducting research.

### EXTINGUISHED
to cause something to stop burning.

# Glossary

**FLASH FLOOD**
a flood that happens very quickly, usually within a couple of hours, after heavy rainfall or the rapid melting of snow.

**FORAGING**
the act of searching for, identifying, and picking wild foods for free.

**GLOBAL POSITIONING SYSTEM**
a satellite-based navigation system that uses radio signals to determine a location on Earth.

**HORIZON**
the line where the sky and the land or sea appear to meet.

**HYDRATED**
having enough water in your body to function properly.

**HYDRATION**
the process of replacing water lost by the body.

**HYPOTHERMIA**
a medical emergency that occurs when a person's body temperature drops below 95°F.

**INSULATION**
the use of materials to prevent the spread of heat.

**KINDLING**
small, dry pieces of wood or other materials used to start a fire.

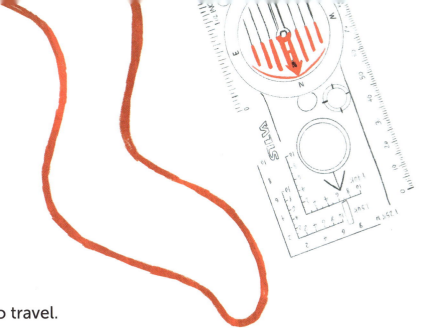

**LICHEN**

a plant-like organism.

**NAVIGATE**

to find the right direction to travel.

**PUNCTURE**

a hole made by a sharp object.

**RAPIDS**

areas of a river where the current is fast and the water is shallow, usually with a broken surface.

**RATIONS**

a fixed amount of food.

**RESPIRATION**

the process by which living things exchange oxygen and carbon dioxide to create energy and remove waste.

**TERRAIN**

the term for the surface features of a specific area of land.

**TINDER**

a dry, flammable material that's used to start fires.

**Warning:** This book is an interactive game book and the suggestions and instructions are provided for general information purposes only. The scenarios included in the book are intended for entertainment and are not intended to be used as a survival guide in the wilds. The publisher would expressly discourage children from carrying out any of the activities in the book in the world outside this book unless accompanied by a responsible adult. Under no circumstances can the author or the publisher accept any liability for any death, injury, or damage arising out of carrying out any activities listed in this book.

**Acquisitions Project Editor** Sara Forster
**Project Art Editor** Jon Hall
**Production Editor** Marc Staples
**Senior Production Controller** Louise Minihane
**Senior Acquisitions Editor** Katy Flint
**Design Manager** Vicky Short
**Art Director** Charlotte Coulais
**Managing Director** Mark Searle

**Designed for DK** by Andrew Watson
**Text copyright** © BVG Global Limited, 2025
**Artwork copyright** © Jake Alexander, 2025

DK would like to thank Ben Elcomb for his editorial consultancy; Rica Dearman and Lisa Davis for proofreading; the team at Bear Grylls Ventures; and Lucy Irvine and Silvia Molteni at Peters Fraser + Dunlop.

First American Edition, 2025
Published in the United States by DK Publishing,
a division of Penguin Random House LLC
1745 Broadway, 20th Floor, New York, NY 10019

Copyright © 2025 Dorling Kindersley Limited
10 9 8 7 6 5 4 3 2 1
001–341638–May/2025

All rights reserved.
Without limiting the rights under the copyright reserved above, no part of this publication may be reproduced, stored in or introduced into a retrieval system, or transmitted, in any form, or by any means (electronic, mechanical, photocopying, recording, or otherwise), without the prior written permission of the copyright owner.
Published in Great Britain by Dorling Kindersley Limited

A catalog record for this book
is available from the Library of Congress.
ISBN: 978-05939-6240-4

DK books are available at special discounts when purchased in bulk for sales promotions, premiums, fund-raising, or educational use. For details, contact: DK Publishing Special Markets,
1745 Broadway, 20th Floor, New York, NY 10019
SpecialSales@dk.com

Printed and bound in China.

www.dk.com

This book was made with Forest Stewardship Council™ certified paper – one small step in DK's commitment to a sustainable future. Learn more at www.dk.com/uk/information/sustainability